SECOND AND ENLARGED EDITION.

The History

OF

THE ANCIENT CITY OF

SUFFOLK.

EDITED AND PUBLISHED BY

S. F. ABBOTT,

Samuel Freeman

TOWN MANSION, LOWESTOFT.

PRICE SIXPENCE.

LOWESTOFT:

GEORGE S. COOK, NELSON PRINTING WORKS.

The History

OF THE

Ancient City of

DUNWICH,

SUFFOLK.

EDITED AND PUBLISHED BY

S. F. ABBOTT,

Town Mansion, Lowestoft.

LOWESTOFT:

George S. Cook, Nelson Printing Works.

DUNWICH.

Where the lone cliff uprears its rugged head,
Where frowns the ruins o'er the silent dead,
Where sweeps the billow on the lonely shore,
Where once the mighty lived, but live no more,
Where proudly frowned the convent's massy wall,
Where rose the gothic tower the stately hall,
Wher: bards proclaimed, and warriors shared the feast,
Where ruled the baron, and where knelt the priest,
There stood the City in its pride—'tis gone—
Mocked at by crumbling pile, and mouldering stone,
And shapeless masses, which the reckless power
Of Time hath hurled from ruined arch and tower !
O'er the lone spot, where shrines and pillared halls
Once gorgeous shone, the clammy lizard crawls ;
O'er the lone spot where yawned the guarded fosse,
Creeps the wild bramble, and the spreading moss :
Oh ! time hath bowed that lordly City's brow
In which the mighty dwelt—where dwell they now ?

How swift, how sure, with dark oblivious wings
Time shrouds the glory of all earthy things !
E'en now he flies—and, as he speeds along
Heeds not the poet, nor the poet's song ;
He sweeps his giant arm—beneath his scythe
The high, the low, the sorrowful, the blithe.
The rich, the poor, the sorrowful, the brave
Crumble to the dust—their heritage the grave ;
And here Time's mightiest, heaviest hand hath been,
How marred the splendour and how changed the scene !
He called his deadliest fiends—in wrath they came,
The furious tempest and the wasting flame,
The raging whirlwind and the gorging sea,
They came old Donewyc, and they spared not thee !

DUNWICH.

OF the antiquity, importance, and wealth of the once magnificent *City of Dunwich*, we have undoubted evidence in the chronicle lore of our country, but it is so much enveloped in the halo of traditionary splendour, that he who attempts to write its history by tracing the path of topographical inquiry must exercise great care lest he be led astray by imaginary light. STOW, in his history, thus describes it "Dunwich, in ancient time, was a city, had brazen gates, fifty-two churches, chapels, religious houses, and hospitals; a king's palace, a bishop's seat, a mayor's mansion and a mint." The veracity, however, which might have revealed itself is almost wholly thrown into oblivion, in consequence of the violent assaults of the ocean; for unlike the ruined cities of the east, whose fragments reveal their former grandeur, Dunwich is wasted, desolate, and void. Its temples and palaces are no more, and its very aspect is lonely and wild, assimilating well with the wreck of its early prosperity. It is evident that our shores have been constantly undergoing changes from the remotest period; headlands have disappeared before the encroachments of the sea, while valleys that have been overrun by the tides of the ocean, have become firm and fertile lands. Hence the

appellation of this place, combined with such truths, leads to
the conclusion that Dunwich in its early days was com-
paratively an inland city, seated on a hill, and watered by
a river of no small dimensions. The tradition therefore of
its forest called Eastwood, which GARDNER says, stretched
out several miles between the town and the ocean, appears
a relation not discreditable in itself, and confirmed, in a
great. measure by the fact that about a century ago the
impetuosity of the waves lay bare the roots of trees,
apparently the extremity of some dense forest, in all proba-
bility the remains of this wood; and even at the present
day, at high tides, the sea throws up, in great abundance,
a congealed submerged matter, in which may be found
roots, branches of trees, nuts, and a vast. quantity of
vegetable substances in pretty good preservation. It cannot
now be determined whether the site of Ancient Dunwich
was a British or Roman station, but evidences of the latter
are incontrovertible, and although the ocean has swallowed
up those gigantic works which invariably mark the labour
and toil of our earliest subjugators, yet the labours of agri-
culture have turned up a variety of implements for domestic
use, and a vast number of coins, in excellent preservation,
which agree in pointing out the spot as being a permanent
Roman Station, the basis of the following Saxon Dommoc-
ceaster. But other proofs are strongly credited and adduce-
able. A Roman road has been distinctly traced, leading
from the heaths which surround this place, entirely across
the county to Bury St. Edmunds; assuredly a station of
great note, if not actually the Villa Fanstini. This line of
communication, which might in primitive times have been a
track-way of the Iceni, has never been obliterated by
ancient records. During the time in which the Saxons
occupied Dunwich, it was used by Sigebert, who planted
christianity there, and was recognised for some considerable
time afterwards as the king's road and the king's highway.
A road, constructed by the Romans, appears to have gone
in a direct line from Dunwich to the "Ad Ansam," through
Burgh, by Woodbridge, traces of which appear in the
modern names of Stratford—a village not far distant from
Saxmundham—and Rackford Bridge, in the parish of Ford-

ley. The latter (says the Rev. SUCKLING) is a corruption of the trackway ford, which preceded the building of a bridge over the little stream which intersects the valley there.

To the arguments derived from this concurrence of roads (says our informant) may be added the existence of a large artificial mound, or tumulus, which crowns the high lands to the south of the town, in the gardens of F. Barne, Esq. This barrow, which is of considerable magnitude, and possibly covers the remains of some illustrious chieftain, may be supposed to have been also used by the Romans for exploratory purposes. To identify, however, the site of Roman Dunwich with the name of any station recorded in Anglo-Roman history, from these general evidences of occupancy, would be a difficult, if not an impossible task; for in no part in England do we find the localities of Roman towns and encampments less satisfactorily fixed than in Suffolk. Theories must remain theories still, open to the fullest discussion; and in this place the fury of the ocean has swept away every considerable remain.

Dunwich was, in the Saxon annals, denominated Domoc; by king Alfred Dommoc-ceaster, or Dvnwyc, from Dyn, a hilly down upon which it was erected, and Wyc, a fort. Its Anglo-Norman name appears to have been Donewyc : It is thus mentioned in old evidences. *In Parochia* Omnium Sanctorum *in Suburbio Civitatis de* Donewyc *juxta Mare.*— [See *Gardner's Historical Account of Dunwich*, p. 4.]

GARDNER, to whom we are indebted for some interesting memorials of the once *Splendid City*, observes that, " We cannot, from any record, justly determine when, or by whom it was founded."—It is reported to have been a station of the Romans, from the circumstance of some of their coins having been found there. Its history, however is not very clearly defined till the time of Sigebert, king of the East Angles.

The sea began its encroachments upon the city at a very early period, for the men of Dunwich required aid of William the Conqueror against the rage of the sea, as they affirmed that it had devoured part of their forest.—[See *Weever's Funeral Monuments*, p. 78].

When the Conqueror's survey was taken, Robert Mallet held Dunwich; at that time there were eleven Bordarii and twenty-four freemen, each holding forty acres of land, one hundred and thirty-six burgesses, and one hundred and seventy-eight poor, and three churches.

The sea having early destroyed its numerous magnificent structures, our Anglo-Norman kings endeavoured to restore Dunwich. Eight or nine churches were built, and it appears to have been in its most flourishing state during the reign of Henry II. GARDNER, in his quaint manner, in relation to that period, thus describes it : " A spacious plot, interspersed with hills and hollows, replenished with buildings fair and magnificent for grandeur, seconded by none in the county, populous and opulent, and of renown."   He also gives a melancholy chronology of the destruction of the aspiring towers of Dunwich from the incursions of the sea.

The oldest map in existence of Dunwich was engraved by GARDNER, in his history.   This map, which was taken in 1587, shows that the church of St. Peter, and Maison-Dieu (or God's House), also the chapel of St. Francis, Black Friars Templar, and the Market-place were then standing.   The period of the highest dignity of Dunwich was in the time of the Saxon era, though not then in its commercial prosperity and wealth.   Dunwich, then called Dunwyk, and Dommoc-ceaster, retained the advantages of its port, and in some measure remained a tenable military station.

In the commencement of the seventh century, when Sigebert was called from the continent to ascend the East Anglian throne, it was selected as the seat of his temporal government, and the nursery of that ecclesiastical establishment whence the spiritual benefits of christianity were first dispensed to his pagan subjects.   The Saxon ecclesiastics were in general men of great piety and learning : amongst them was the venerable Bede, born A.D. 673, whose history of the Anglo-Saxon Church is so highly valued.   A palace was raised by the king for his residence, and a church, or churches founded by Felix, upon whom the episcopal dignity was conferred.

Thou sea-worn city !—in the times of old,
Ere winds and waves had torn thee from thy hold,
Then was the day-spring of thy glory bright,
When thy brave Sigebert spread the heavenly light
Of sacred learning o'er his happy realm,
Man's weal his compass, truth divine his helm !
Then thy good bishop, noble Felix, came
To swell thy glory, to exalt thy fame.
Yes ! in thy holy temple first were taught
Those won'drous truths, above the power of thought,
That o'er East Anglia's joyful bound spread wide,
The glorious light to comfort and to guide
The soul-benighted mortal on his way,
Through shade: of death to everlasting day.

We must not suffer ourselves to be led away by the
imaginary magnificence of these buildings, which could have
been but the rude fabrics of the early Saxons, most probably
constructed of timber, or, if of more durable materials,
selected without doubt from the ruins of the Roman works.
But to date the exact period of Felix's first establishment
at Dunwich would be ficticious, being involved in much
uncertainty. BEDE places it in the year 630 ; but the
Saxons in their chronicles, and other historians, in 635, or
some little time after; and as Felix received his consecration
from Honorius, Archbishop of Canterbury, who was not
himself elevated from Lincoln to that high dignity before
the year 643, the last date appears the most creditable. To
reconcile ourselves to these disputes, let us suppose that
Felix, who was a Burgundian priest, brought over by Sigebert, preached the doctrine of christianity to his pagan
subjects at Dunwich on his first arrival in 630, but he was
not raised to that high office of bishop till a few years later,
when the truths by his activity, had spread far and wide.

The reign of Sigebert, as history informs us, was but of
short duration, having terminated three years after its commencement, being persuaded by Fursœus, a Scot, to prefer a
cowl to a crown, he was shorn a monk at Cnobhersburgh
(now called Burgh Castle) near Great Yarmouth. Egric, his
kinsman, succeeded him on the throne, who was continually
harassed by the Mercians, under Penda their king, and
reduced to such great straits, that all means proved unsuc-

cessful in animating the army to face the enemy, without
the presence of their favourite monarch, who against his
inclinations was dragged from his cell to the camp, bearing
for his arms only a white wand, where he, together with
Egric, fell victims to that avaricious monarch, A.D. 642.

Dunwich being the chief town, it consequently assisted
Sigebert and Egric in their wars with Penda, and afterwards
Anna, against the same king, whom historians affirm was
slain with his son Ferminas, and interred in the church at
Blythborough.   I have seen, says GARDNER, three brass
coins of the same stamp found at Dunwich, one of them
with Anna legible, a sketch of which he has given in the
history of that place.   The short period of Sigebert's reign
was not marked with inactivity or useless government ; it is
said he laboured zealously for the promotion of the spiritual and temporal welfare of his subjects.   BEAL informs us
that he was so charmed with the progress of literature on
the continent, that he founded a school in his dominions,
after the models he had seen, in which the rudiments of
grammar and the sciences were taught by learned men,
whom he had invited from France.   This infant establishment (says SMITH in his notes on BEDE's " Eccl. History,")
was fixed at Dunwich, and formed the germ whence the
University of Cambridge sprouted.   It is certain that Sigebert and Felix have the honour of giving a settled establishment of christianity in these dominions ; churches and
monastries were built and endowed ; that at Bedericksworth,
now called Bury St. Edmunds, rearing in after days its
towers amidst the proudest and most wealthy of the land.
GODWINUS, in his history, relates that Felix presided over
his diocese till the day of his death, which occured on the
8th March, 647.   LELAND says he was buried at Dunwich ;
if so, it is certain that he was exhumed, and his remains
deposited at Soham, in his abbey which he had founded ;
and where they remained but for short duration, being again
removed in Canute's reign, to the Abbey of Ramsey.   In
this church the ashes of this prelate were enshrined with
splendour, and his name canonized as the first saint of the
eastern part of England.   He was succeeded by Thomas in

his bishopric, who is called by GODWINUS his deacon, and was followed in that chair by Boniface, and Bisus, or Bosa..

When old age and infirmities oppressed this latter prelate (says BEDE) he divided his diocese into two, retaining that of Dunwich. which was to embrace Suffolk and the other see at North Elmham, in Norfolk. Eleven prelates succeeded him at Dunwich, viz. :—1. Acca (or Etta). 2. Astwolph. 3. Eadferth, consecrated in 734. 4. Cuthwin. 5. Aiberth. 6. Eglaf. 7. Headred. 8. Alsin (Æfun', buried at Dunwich. 9. Tidferth. 10. Weremund. 11. Wibred. In the person of the last-named bishop, the bishoprics of Dunwich and North Elnham were united in the year 870, or thereabouts. Thus Dunwich sank from its episcopal rank, from which it had only emerged to that of a rural deanery. Although the seat of the bishopric was thus removed from Suffolk, it continued to enjoy some shadow of the episcopal dignity for several hundred years after; and although Dunwich was pre eminent during the middle period of the Saxons, in dignity and rank, it is evident that it was in a declining state in the reign of Edward the Confessor. The sea had swept away its regal palace and episcopal seat, and wasted an entire *carucute* of land, as shown by Domesday book. It was a burgh however, and possessed 120 burgesses; but it is very remarkable, considering it to have been so long the seat of a bishopric, that it contained only one church. This, without doubt, was founded by the good bishop Felix, and was dedicated to him. The town, at that period, paid ten pounds to the crown. Changes of a very important nature however took place in the short interval which elapsed between the reign of the Confessor and the Conqueror's survey. At this last period, its burgesses amounted•to 236, and the number of poor persons in the town amounted to 178. The churches were three in number, and the customary rent amounted to £50 and 60,000 herrings by gift. The improved condition of Dunwich at this juncture, is due to one, Robert Mallett, a man of great influence, and of Norman extraction, on whom this place was bestowed by the last-named monarch. In Domesday book, in the time of Edward the Confessor, it appears that they had no money changers, or bankers, at Dunwich, but one at Blythborough. The real condition of Dunwich at this period may be estimated by contrasting its Domesday return with those of other towns in Suffolk, made in the same record. The retainers of the abbey of Bury, in the Confessor's reign, exclusive of the monks, were 310. The burgesses of Ipswich amounted to 538, and ten churches. Sudbury, in the same monarch's reign had 118, and a richly endowed church, and, it is said, a mint; which latter privilege (says the Rev. SUCKLING) was never conferred on Dunwich, although GARDNER affirms it in his historical account of that place. If it once possessed a mint, it doubtless must have been in the Saxon era, when kings and bishops resided in it; but no one of the present day ever saw or heard of a Saxon or any other coin stamped at Dunwich.

LEAK says that arched coins of Henry VI. were minted at Dunwich, but he is evidently in error; and what he reads as "Cite de Denwyk" should have been "Everwyk" (or York); the one engraved by GARDNER may possibly have been a blundered penny of Edward IV. struck at Durham.

Robert Mallett being deprived of his estates, and banished the kingdom, Dunwich came to the crown. The ancient chronicler, William of Newbury, observes that a blank presents itself in the history of Dunwich, till the reign of Henry II., when it emerged to the very heighth of its prosperity, being a town of great note, abounding with much riches and sundry kinds of merchandize. The rent of the fee-farm to the crown was now elevated to £120 and one mark (or £120 13s. 4d.) and 24,000 herrings. It paid also £133 6s. 8d. as an aid on the marriage to Maud, daughter to King Henry. II Ipswich paid but £53 6s. 8d., a proof of its rapid stride in commercial affairs. BLOMFIELD says that at the commencement of the unnatural war, waged by Prince Henry and his brother against their father, King Henry II., the mercenary troops, commanded by the Earl of Leicester, appeared off the Suffolk coast, and are supposed to have made an unsuccessful attempt to disembark at Dunwich, before they affected their landing at

Walton, in 1173, September 21st; the said earl joined Hugh Bygod at Framlingham Castle, where he stayed some time; they received fresh troops from France, marched to Ipswich, and being joined by more forces of Earl Bygod's, directed their course to Hawley Castle, belonging to Ralp' Brot, which they burnt to the ground; then returned to Framlingham, at which time the Countess of Leicester arriving at Orford with fresh supplies, joined them and then marched to Norwich, and overran the counties of Suffolk and Norfolk, and reduced them to the obedience of the new king; but sitting down before Dunwich, and reconnoitring the situation strength, and difficult access of the place, despairing of success, they suspended their dangerous enterprise of assaulting it, and willingly, or (as HOLLAND says) by compulsion, retired with their army into Leicestershire.

This statement is evidently correct, as it appears by a manuscript in the British Museum, entitled, "A description of the towne of Dunwich," and dated August, 1590. This place was certainly strongly fortified at this time, and capable of offering a vigorous resistance, as is also shown by various other documents which are too long to be introduced into this small volume. GARDNER relates in his history, that on Westleton Heath, not two miles from Dunwich, are remains of these fortifications, thrown up by Leicester when he beseiged that town, and which may be seen to the present day. STOW says that the oldest of the inhabitants of this neighbourhood report that Dunwich in ancient times was a city surrounded by a stone wall and brazen gates. But in a manuscript no illusion to a stone wall or brazen gates appears; from which we may fairly conclude is one of the traditionary fictions connected with this place. Dunwich was fined in the reign of Richard I. 1,060 marks; Orford 15, Ipswich 200, and Yarmouth the same sum, for supplying (as GARDNER says) the Flemmings with corn. Dunwich was firmly attached to the interests of King John, during the memorable struggle of the Barons, for the enforcement of Magna Charta, and fitted out several ships to substantiate his power. These measuses led to reprisals on the part of the king's enemies, for the barons with the French made great havoc in this country, extorting from Dunwich, to avoid a direption, immense sums of money.

In consequence of the adherence of the townsmen of Dunwich to the king's interests, he created the town a free borough with *soc* and *sac;* exempting it from certain tolls and customs, and among the rest wreck and lagan,—that is, goods lying at the bottom of the sea, lost by shipwreck, which by the ancient laws belonged to the Lord Admiral. This is (says the Rev. SUCKLING) doubtless the charter for which the burgesses paid 200 marks and 5000 cels. It must be remarked (says our informant), *however*, that it exempts them only from wreck and lagan throughout the realm, instead of granting them the same, as GARDNER has incorrectly stated. King John remitted the burgesses £40 rent of their fee-farm, and in after years confirmed his first charter, vesting the government of the town in a mayor and four bailiffs, or sheriffs, in place of the portreeves, who had hitherto exercised the municipal authority. For these favours the town gave him in addition to their former payments, 300 marks in money, and ten falcons, and five girfalcons. In 1216 Dunwich was first governed by mayors and bailiffs, and continued so for 130 years, terminating in the twentieth year of the reign of Edward III., viz :—1346. A long list appears in GARDNER's history of these corporate dignities. The town has been subsequently governed by two bailiffs, who act as chief magistrates, assisted by a recorder and other officers. The grants of King John to the town were confirmed by his son, Henry III., in the fourteenth and fortieth years of his reign. He also made a further abatement of £20 per annum in the fee-farm rent of the town, and gave them £47 10s. to remove and repair their port. We may date the decline of the commercial prosperity of Dunwich at this period, having been brought about by the encroachments of the ocean, which have gradually reduced it from a populous and flourishing port to a mean and impoverished village ; yet it furnished the king with forty ships when required, for his own use, as it appears from Lansdowne's M.SS. In the reign of Edward I., Dunwich maintained, besides 11 ships of war, 16 fair ships, 20 barks trading to the North Seas, and 24 small boats for the home fishery. In the 24th year of this reign, Dunwich built for the defence of the realm 11 ships of war furnished with munition, carrying 72 men each. These ships, sailing from Plymouth with the Earls of Leicester and Lancaster, to the coast of Gascony, they served the king free of expense, and had four ships taken and destroyed by the enemy, valued at £200. No charter of privilege was granted to Dunwich by Edward II., but he issued a mandate to John Howard, sheriff of Suffolk, prohibiting the sale of goods at the new port, except at the ancient market-place at Dunwich. Gardner says in the first year of King Edward III. the old port of Dunwich was rendered quite useless by the violence of the sea, and in 1328 was so choked up by the north-east winds, that all means for its recovery proved ineffectual. This monarch, in the third year of his reign, was a great benefactor to the town, but nothing could maintain its prosperity, which now rapidly declined; notwithstanding, in 1347 it sent six ships for the king against Calais. About this period a great part of the town, and upwards of 400 houses, which paid rent to the fee farm, with divers shops and wind-mills, were destroyed by the sea; the fee-farm rent was consequently reduced to £14 10s. 9d. GARDNER says, that in addition to the church of St. Felix, with a cell of monks, which had long been lost, the churches of St. Leonord, St. Martin, and St. Nicholas, were now overthrown by the sea, and in 1485, the shore was washed away close to the convent of Black Friars. Henry the VI. reduced the fee-farm rent to £12 2s. 1d. The first known charter granted to the burgesses of Dunwich was in the reign of Edward IV., for services done to that monarch. The town chest of Dunwich possesses no original charters, nor even transcripts of charters, granted to the burgesses there by the kings of England of any period, or by any earl of the shire, or lord of the city, borough, or town. The suppression of the religious houses, with the previous existing evils, hastened its decay. Queen Elizabeth, in the first year of her reign, gave the town a charter of confirmation, "a princely gift," which, as the poet says, fell "like sun beams on the blasted blossoms," for the place was now

reduced to less than one-quarter of its original size. The
church of St. John the Baptist was taken down in 1540 ;
several of its chapels, with Gilden Gate and South Gate,
were now overthrown by the sea ; in 1570 it suffered considerable damage. Her majesty, in consideration of these
aggrievances, lent the town a sum of money, which she
obtained by the sale of the bells, lead, etc., of Ingate
Church in Beccles, together with the sale of lead, etc., from
Kessingland Church. It is thought that STOW was the
author of a very curious and circumstantial manuscript, now
in the British Museum, but no name is appended to it ; it
runs thus : "Excited by curiosity I visited this place, where
I beheld the remains of the ramparts, some tokens of
Middle Gate, the foundations of down-fallen edifices, and
tottering fragments of noble structures, remains of the dead
exposed, and naked walls divested of the ground about
them, by the waves of the sea ; divers coins, several mill
hills ; and part of the old key." This was written in the
year 1573. This account (says the Rev. SUCKLING) is
dedicated to " Master Deye," who must have been, I think,
the John Day (or Deye) who was born in Dunwich in the
beginning of the 16th century, and is celebrated as the first
English printer who employed a Saxon type. Day died in
1584, and was buried at Bradley in Suffolk. In an old chest,
in the Town Hall is a mace of silver, weighing eleven
ounces and three-quarters, and in length ten inches and a
half, made in the shape of an arrow ; upon the broad end,
or head, of which are engraved the royal arms, quartered
with those of the borough. The corporation also possesses
an ancient silver badge, on which are the town arms. In
1589 the port of Dunwich was again choked by the violence
of the north-east winds; it was then called "Hummers-
ston's Cut," and appears to have been difficult of access,
and where, doubtless, numbers have perished.

The original map (or " platt ") mentioned by AGAS, in his
report of Dunwich, is not known where deposited. VIRTUE
had seen on a large skin of vellum, a plan of the town and
boundaries of Dunwich, with its churches, adjacent villages,
&c., and several remarks made by Radulphus Agas in 1589.

Undoubtedly this is the one from which GARDNER engraved his, as mentioned in our preceding pages, but he dates it 1587.

In 1608, the high road to the beach was devoured by the sea ; the foundations of the Knights Templars soon after disappeared ; and in 1677, the sea reached the Market Place, when the inhabitants, anticipating the destruction of the place, took down the market cross and sold the lead. Three years later, all the buildings north of Maison-Dieu Lane were demolished. The fee-farm rent, in consideration of the poverty of the town, King Charles II. reduced to £7 2s. 1d. per annum ; in 1705, Dunwich stood indebted to the crown £1260, for the arrears of 21 years at £60 per annum. A new charter was granted to the town in the reign of William and Mary, under which the present corporation exists. It confirms all former charters, and restores all the rights and privileges which had been wrestled from them by the surrender of their charters in the reigns of Charles II. and James II.

Under the old charters the borough of Dunwich was entitled to, and to take all wreck found on the beach, from the South Pier of Southwold Harbour on the north, to the Cachecliff on the south. This wreck of sea restored to Dunwich was no invaluable privilege, for about 60 years since, a large quantity of wine was thus obtained ; and in 1803, as much tallow as was sold for £2,000. In 1702 the sea extended its dominion to St. Peter's Church, which was obliged to be taken down ; the Town Hall suffered the same fate. In 1715 the Jail was undermined, and in 1729, the utmost bounds of St. Peter's Cemetery gave way to the insulting waves. GARDNER records an awful storm which took place here in December, 1740 : "The wind blowing very hard about N.E., a continuance for several days occasioned great seas, doing much damage on the coast during that time, by inundations, breaking down the banks, and overflowing many marshes, etc. The same effects thereof were severely felt by Dunwich, when a great deal of its cliffs were washed away, with the remains of St. Nicholas's churchyard, and the great road heretofore leading into the

town from the quay, leaving several naked wells, tokens of
several ancient buildings, and from Maison-Dieu Lane
northwards, a continued scene of confusion.   Part of the
old quay, built with stone, lay bare, making canals across
the beach, through which the river had communications
with the sea, to the hinderance of the people on foot travel-
ling that way, for some days.   King's Holms (alias
Leonard's Marsh) heretofore valued at £200, and then at
£100 per annum, was laid under water, and much shingle
and sand thrown thereon from off the beach, rendering it
ever since of little value : much of the pasture and arable
land destroyed.   The sea raged with such fury that Cock
and Hen Hills, which the preceding summer were upwards
of 40 feet high, and in the winter partially washed away,
this year had their heads levelled with their bases, and the
ground above them so rent and torn, that the foundation of
St. Francis' Chapel, which was laid between the said hills,
was discovered.   Where, besides the ruins of the walls,
were five round stones near of a bigness : the dimensions
of which I took were four feet the diameter, and near two
the thickness.   There was likewise a circle of large stumps
of piles, about twenty-four feet circumference.   The bounds
of the cemetery were naked, within which the secret
repositories of the dead were exposed to open view ; several
skeletons on the ouze divested of their coverings, some
lying in pretty good order, others interrupted and scattered,
as the surges carried them.   · Also a stone coffin, wherein
were human bones, covered with tiles. Before a conveniency
offered for removing the coffin, it was broken in two pieces
by the violence of the sea, which now serve for 'steps at
each foot of Deering Bridge."   At the same time, and
near the chapel, the pipes of an acqueduct were found, some
of lead, others of grey earth, like that of some urns.

In the year 1740, as the men of Dunwich were digging a
trench near their old port across the beach, to make a water-
gang to drain their marshes and low grounds they happened
on a stone wall cemented exceeding strong, which was part
of their *old quay ;* and near that, on a well, both of which
I saw as they were working, at which time several pieces of

old coins and other curiosities were found." These are represented in a rude cut in GARDNER's work, and are,—1st, a bodkin, or pin, with a silver head; 2nd, a very curious ancient key with double wards; and 3rd, part of an old brass lock, etc.

No considerable encroachments of the sea have taken place at Dunwich for about 70 years past. In 1754, when GARDNER wrote his history, divine service was performed once a fortnight in All Saints' Church, which was then the only sacred edifice in use. This was, however, discontinued altogether about the period just mentioned, when the last great inroad of the sea was made on Dunwich.

The inhabitants, for fear, dismantled their last remaining temple, or as a modern writer informs us, it was not that alone, but the value of the bells and lead went far towards effecting this desecration. Dunwich, as a borough, sent burgesses to Parliament by prescription, and not by charter, so it appears by the town records. Its first members were Thomas Torold and William Sacor, who assisted in the Parliament held at York, in the 23rd of Edward I.

It was disfranchised by the "Act to amend the representation of the people of England and Wales," passed on the 7th of June, 1832. The members were elected in the old Town House (or Hall), afterwards used as a schoolroom. Here they were chaired, and carried in procession up and down the road before its front, for about a hundred yards; and in it the election feasts were formerly kept. In this low and not imposing apartment, stood an old Dutch iron-bound chest, painted with green, and decorated with flowers of various kinds, and six sea views, and landscapes of great antiquity on its frontage; in this chest were deposited the town records, secured by five springs and two locks, of massive iron workmanship. It contains a small octavo book of about two hundred pages, commencing about the reign of Henry IV. In the first page is written the charter of Henry IV. It seems to be a book of the corporate proceedings, and records, presentments, lists of burgesses, freemen, etc.

Much curious, if not important matter, is probably contained in this book, which is not known by any particular
name, nor has it any index, or table of contents.   In the
chest is also a register book, containing the proceedings of
the assemblies, common halls, and other meetings relating
to the corporation business, from the 27th October, 1595, to
the 17th June, 1629.   There is a second book of similar
import, dated from the 11th of December, 1627, to 1650,
and a third of the same description, from the 6th of Decem-
1654, to July 18th, 1673.   This last gives at some length,
an account of the proceedings between King Charles I. and
his Parliament, and the arguments used in the conference
between the two Houses, etc.   The present corporation are
now the lords of the manor, and pay no fine whatever, and
hold it by a perpetual tenure.   What remains of the ancient
boundaries of Dunwich forms a long narrow strip of land,
and extends about five miles and a half in length, from the
south Pier of Southwold Haven to Cachecliff, and contains
1360 acres, 38 perches.   The population of Dunwich in
olden times it is difficult to ascertain.   In the reign of
Queen Elizabeth, the population, including all ranks and
conditions, was under 750; and in 1754 there were but 35
houses, and about 100 inhabitants.

In 1841, the population of Dunwich amounted to 237,
and in 1851, to 296 souls.   In the height of its prosperity,
it had a daily market, which declined as the borough
decreased to one weekly, on Saturday; but this, for many
years past has been quite disused.   St. Leonard's fair was
also held in that parish on the 5th, 6th, and 7th days of
November.

South of the town stands the spacious and elegant
Elizabethian mansion of Frederick Barne, Esq.   In this
gentleman's collection of the antiquities of ancient Dunwich,
is a coin of Claudius Nero, and a gold angel of
Edward IV. in good preservation ; also a large brass, a
curious head and bust of a figure, cast in the mixed metal
of which the celts are composed, and thought by that
gentleman to have formed a hammer; and a gold ring, found
by a labourer, hoeing turnips, on which is inscribed, "Time

trieth realitie." This gentleman's predecessors had a valuable cabinet of curiosities connected with this place, but it is now dispersed, and not even a catalogue left behind; a vast quantity of ancient coins, keys, ancient stoups, or basins, and stones with ancient mouldings carved upon them have been dredged up at Dunwich.

We must not omit to notice the lovely little white rose, called the Dunwich rose. It grows plentifully over the neighbouring district, and delights most in the sandy lands of Dunwich. It is a species of Scotch rose, and its delicious perfume soon discovers itself to the traveller; it blooms during the whole of the rose season. Its charms are graphically described by the Suffolk poet, James Bird :—

> There smiles the Dunwich rose with spotless blossom,
> White, pure, and soft, as in the cygnet's bosom.
> This decks the stern and sterile cliff and throws
> O'er its rugged brow new beauty when it grows,
> Gives its proud ruggedness an aspect fair,
> Like hope that brightens on the brow of care.

Tradition says, this floweret was originally planted here and cultivated by the monks. It has given name to a once popular air, known as "Dunwich Roses."

The beautiful major sea-convolvulus may be found near the boat-house of F. Barne, Esq., on the beach. This plant, which is extremely rare, delights in the loosest sand and shingle, has small yellow-green leaves and a delicate pink blossom of a noble size, being much larger than the common major convolvulus, and marked with five crimson velvet stripes. Unlike that charming flower, it does not climb, but contents itself with lifting its blossom not more than two inches above the sand.

The Churches and Religious Houses.

The existence of 52 churches in Dunwich, says the Rev. SUCKLING, is one of those fictions with which tradition and romance have invested its history. In the time of Edward the Confessor, one church only, dedicated to Felix, the first bishop of the see, was then subsisting. In this church Felix was interred, although his remains were afterwards exhumed, as before mentioned. At the Norman Survey the number of churches had increased to three, which was afterwards extended to six, besides the hospital of St. James, and several chapels and alms-houses. These six churches were added to the possessions of the priory at Eye, by Robert Mallett, lord of the manor of Dunwich; they were St. Leonard, St. John Baptist, St. Martin, St. Nicholas, St. Peter, and All Saints; those of St. Michael, and St. Bartholomew, says the register of Eye, were swallowed up by the sea before the year 1331; the last two are mentioned in no other record.

The Church of St. Leonard.

The church is thought by GARDNER to have stood eastward of St. John's, and to have been early lost by the ocean; he also gives the representation of an oblong seal of "Richard, Priest of St. Linnart," dated 1334. In 1270, Roger Crystepen gave a piece of land, in this parish, to the Priory and Convent of Eye, for the good of his soul, etc. This church was appropriated to the Priory of Eye.

The Church of St. John Baptist.

This edifice was large, and stood by the great market-place, in the centre of the town. In 1510, a jetty was built before it to arrest the assaults of the ocean. In 1537, it must have been in a precarious situation, as the parishioners pulled it down three years afterwards, to save the materials from falling over the cliff. In the chancel, says WEEVER, was a large grave-stone which, when raised, discovered a stone coffin, wherein lay the corpse of a man, which fell to dust when stirred. Upon his legs were a pair of boots piked like crakows; and on his breast stood two challices of coarse metal. He was thought to have been a bishop of Dunwich. TANNER informs us, in this church were the images of St. John Baptist, Mary Magdalene, and Anne, the mother of the Virgin Mary, with the guilds of St. John Baptist and St. Catharine. In this church several persons of distinction were interred; and left several sums of money for repairs, etc. The first vicar of this church was Joes de Laugton, in 1340, and the last was William Syward, in 1537.

The Church of St. Martin.

This benifice was a rectory, and is thought to have stood on the east side of the town. 1308, Joes de Dereby was rector: and in 1335, Nicholas de Specteshall. GARDNER mentions a William de Blithborough, sub-deacon, as rector of this church, in 1318; but Mr. SUCKLING thinks it incorrect, having followed the list of incumbents here from the institution books at Norwich.

The Church of St. Nicholas.

This church was a cruciform structure and a rectory, and is said by GARDNER to have stood 20 rods south-east of the convent of Black Friars. This church, according to the old manuscript account of Dunwich, belonged to the largest parish in the town. It had no instititution to the benefice after the year 1352, soon after which period it was devoured by the sea. A portion of it, however, for some years formed the key-stone of a window in a house belonging to the town, and is now preserved as a relic of by-gone days, by J. Gooding, Esq., of Southwold. It was thus inscribed:—Sce Nicholae ora pro nobis. In 1301, Alexandra' de Beccles was rector; and in 1352, Thomas...... de Sterston. The utmost bounds of this cemetery were washed away by the sea, in 1740.

The Church of St. Peter.

This church was a rectory, and stood, according to GARDNER, sixty rods north-east of All Saints. It was visited on the 6th of April, 1643, by DOWSING, whose journal contains the following notice of "superstitious pictures and ornaments" which he found therein:—"Dunwich, St. Peter's parish, sixty-three cherubims, sixty at least of Jesus written in capital letters on the roof, and forty superstitious pictures, and a cross on the top of the steeple. All was promised by the churchwardens to be done."

This church by reason of the proximity of the sea, which daily threatened its overthrow, was by the agreement of the parishioners, in 1702, striped of its lead, timber, bells, and other materials, the walls only remaining, which tumbled over the cliff as the waves undermined them. John Deye, the printer, was a native of this parish.

In the north aisle of this church was an altar dedicated to St. Nicholas, the favourite and patron saint of fishermen. The church-yard of this parish was swallowed up by the sea not more than twenty years before GARDNER wrote his history, when the "remains of the dead were seen sticking on the sides of the cliff. In 1303, Robert de Creike was rector, and in 1606, Clement Bacon. This church had many benefactors, who were interred within its walls.

The Church of All Saints.

This church is the only sacred fabric in the town of which any portion remains, except a new chapel, which will be presently described; it was dismantled about 73 years since by the parishioners, for the sake of the bells and lead. It is a mean structure, and built with flint and freestone; it failed, however, to escape the visit of DOWSING, who tells us he found at "Allhallows, thirty superstitious pictures, and twenty-eight cherubims, and a cross on the chancel. According to its shafts, it was built about 1350; several benefactors gave to the building a new aisle, and covering the same. It must soon after 1535 have been appropriated to the corporation of the town, for GARDNER says, "in this aisle were magisterial seats, decorated with curious carved work, resembling them in Southwold church; the windows adorned with painted glass, which the glazier without regard to it, or the founder, brake to pieces." The north aisle was pulled down by faculty in 1725. The lead of the roof, with other materials, were sold by John Shipman and Francis Swatman, churchwardens, and the grave-stones employed in the foundations of the wall, then raised to block up the ancient arches. Many plates of brass, inscribed to the memory of persons interred within the aisle were embezzled and sold. In 1451, the great east window was put in, as John Lewk, by his will, gave 6s. 8d. to complete the same. This church, with the exception of the north aisle, was entire and in use, in GARDNER'S time. He thus describes it :—" All Saints' Church is the only one in being where divine service is celebrated, from Lady-day to Michaelmas, once a fortnight, and monthly the succeeding half-year, the minister's stipend not exceeding £12 by the year, exclusive of a small provisional allowance for refreshment, in consideration of his journey thither. The inside walls, especially the chancel, are infected with an incurable spreading leprosy."

The tower, built of flint and free-stones,· with various decorations, is old but pretty strong, and indifferently handsome, crowned with a battlement, each angle supporting an angel, representing Gabriel, Michael, Raphael, and Uriel. It is deprived of a· clock, which formerly it enjoyed, but possesses three bells ; the first, or little bell, cast in 1725 ; the second, in 1678 ; and the third in 1626." Two monumental inscriptions were remaining in the church in 1754, on brass plates, one with the effigies of a man and woman, with one son and six daughters, to the memory of Thomas Cooper, 1576 ; the other to the memory of Robert Spashett, 1624 ; and many others on stones, but of whom no vestiges are left.

The church-yard of all Saints is still occasionally used as a burial place, there being many grave-stones near the west wall of a recent date. The first chaplain of All Saints' Church was Rogerus Bettys ; the last, in 1628, was Robert Pabie.

The new Chapel of St. James.

This neat and substantial structure is built within the

grounds formerly belonging to the Hospital of St. James ; through the munificence of the Barne family it was erected. It measures, internally, sixty two feet in length, by twenty-two feet in width. It is a perpetual curacy, in the gift of F. Barne, Esq., but is not endowed with, or possessed of, any glebe lands, messuages, tenements, tithes, or portions of tithes whatever ; but has been recently augmented by £400 of Queen Anne's bounty money. The earliest register here commences in 1672, and was brought from the old church of All Saints.

It contains a mural monument to Michael Barne, Esq., of Sotterly, representative of the borough of Dunwich in four successive Parliaments, and formerly Lieutenant-Colonel of the 7th (or Queen's Own) Regiment of Light Dragoons, in which he served as commandant, under His Royal Highness the Duke of York, during the campaign of 1793 and 1794, in the Netherlands, and in the expedition to the Helder, in 1799. By his care—and principally by the aid of his liberal contributions—this chapel was erected, in the year 1830. He died June 19th, 1837, and was interred in a vault erected in that portion of the old Hospital of St. James, called the temple. The first curate of St. James' Chapel was Robert Howlett, in 1832.

The Chapels

were dedicated to St. Anthony, St. Francis, and St. Katherine. The site of the former was swallowed up by the sea very early, and it is unknown in what part of the town it stood. St. Francis was situated between Cock and Hen Hills, and seems to have survived the fury of the ocean, to share in the general dissolution of monastic establishments. St. Katharine's chapel stood in the parish of St. John, and shared the same fate as that of St. Francis.

The Preceptory of the Knights Templars.

Of the exact time at which the knights settled at Dunwich there is no record, but their house was certainly in existence here in the reign of King John, as shown by the charter rolls; also by another in the reign of Henry III. The church of this establishment is described as a fine structure, " vaulted over and the aisles all leaded." " It stood " (says GARDNER), near Middle-gate Street, having Duck Street (Duke Sreet ?) on the north, and Covent Garden on the south, distant from All Saints about fifty-five rods." Elizabeth, daughter of Thomas Knivett, marrying Sir John Rous, at Henham, carried the temple manor, etc., into that family. John Rous, Esq., sold them to Charles Long, Esq., who conveyed them to Miles Barne, Esq., from whom they have descended to Frederick Barne, Esq., of Grey Friars, Dunwich. The lordship is now styled " The Manor of the Temple and the Holy Virgin." Its demesnes have been almost entirely swallowed up by the sea ; two acres only remain.

The Convent of Franciscan Friars.

They are called also Grey Friars and Friar Minors. Of the history of this establishment, whose shattered pile forms the most attractive object in the " ruined city," very little has descended to us. The sea has spared its site, but its records are scattered or destroyed. WEEVER says :—it was founded by Richard Fitz John and Alice; afterwards augmented by Henry III. This friary plot contains upwards of seven acres of land, encompassed by a stone wall, and had three gates : one eastward, now quite demolished, and two westward, whose arches continue pretty firm, and are mantled with ivy in rich luxuriance, giving a charm to its crumbling portals.

Through the large gateway is seen the shattered fabric of All Saints' Church, in grey and sober distance ; and on passing beneath its arch, the eye is arrested by a mass of ruins on the right, the loftiest parts of which formed perhaps portion of the conventual church. Part of these ruins was appropriated to a substantial residence, and a second portion fitted up as a hall, or chambers, for the transaction of corporation business, and another part served as a jail,

against which was reared a mighty screen of brickwork,
which GARDNER describes as affording a "handsome
prospect ;" this was standing in 1780 ; but these deformities
have for some time been removed, and the whole site preserved with much laudable care.   This conventual church
had many benefactors, who were interred within its walls.
GARDNER says, the heart of Dame Hawise Poynings was
buried here ; and he gives the representation of the circular
part of a buckle, or fibula of brass, found by a workman
in removing some earth from within the walls of the Grey
Friars.   It laid on the top of a small earthen vessel, which
he broke into fragments, thinking it contained treasure.
There is reason to believe that it was the very urn in which
had been deposited the heart of this dame.   The circum-
scription was of a usual character : 𝔄𝔟𝔢 𝔐𝔞𝔯𝔦𝔞 𝔤𝔯𝔞𝔠𝔦𝔞
𝔭𝔩𝔢𝔫𝔞.

Three fine seals belonging to this house have been found ;
one is engraved by Mr. SUCKLING, and the other by GARD-
NER ; the third is not described.   The site of the Friars
Minors at Dunwich is now the property of F. Barne, Esq.

The Convent of Dominican or Black Friars.

This order of monks, who are called also Friars Preachers,
was instituted in 1206, and came to England in 1221. The
precise period when they arrived at Dunwich is not known,
but it is supposed soon after the latter date.   The founder
of this house at Dunwich was Sir Roger de Holishe, Knight,
who was interred in this church.   The site of this establishment was one hundred-and-twenty rods from Grey Friars,
and was nearly destroyed by the sea before 1384. GARDNER
gives a long list of persons of note who were interred within its walls, but whose bones, with the church and edifices,
now lay under the insulting waves of the sea.

The Common (or Convent) Garden, mentioned by GARDNER,
as abutting upon Sea Field, might have been the garden
once attached to this monastry.   He informs us that as the
sea made encroachments upon it many human bones were
discovered, and that part was washed away in the winter of
1740,

The Hospitals.

The principal of these was that dedicated to St. James, the Elder Apostle, and appropriated to the reception of lepers. BLOOMFIELD, the Norfolk historian, says, that John, Earl of Moreton, and afterwards King of England, was the founder ; but MARTIN ascribes its foundation to Walter de Riboff, who appears rather as its principal benefactor, having endowed both the church and the hospltals with consider- able revenues. The society consisted of a master and several leprous brethren and sisters. The church of this hospital is described as " a great one, and a fair large one, after the old fashion, and divers tenements, houses, and lands, to the same belonging, to the use of the poor sick and impotent people there." It was of simple form, and without aisles, but comprising the tripartite division of nave, chancel, and sanctum sanctorum, like the primitive churches of the East. Its length was one hundred and seven feet seven inches, and its breadth twenty feet nine inches. The sides were ornamented with small interesting arches, pecu- liar to Saxon and Norman architecture. The revenues of this hospital, which were formerly very considerable, fell in- to decay through the mismanagement of " evilly-disposed covetous persons, who did sell away divers lands and rents from the said hospital." In 1739 it had dwindled to £26 per annum, and in 1754 to £21 19s. 8d. Of this church, the roofless walls only remain. On the 30th January, 1774 (says GARDNER) the repository of relics belonging to this church, which had probably been concealed at the Reforma- tion, was discovered in the sanctum sanctorum, and broken open, near which (continues our informant), as old people report, was the portraiture of a man, which continued there until the celebration of divine service ceased, which was about the year 1685, when the church fell into decay, and everything therein was destroyed. This image, probably of the original founder of the church, or of St. James the patron saint, escaped the notice of DOWSING and our early reformers.

The seal of this hospital was circular and large. Legend :
𝕾𝖆𝖌𝖆𝖑 𝕾𝖆𝖈𝖙 𝕵𝖆𝖈𝖔𝖇.........𝕯𝖔𝖓𝖜𝖎𝖏.

Maison Dieu

(Or God's house) was dedicated to the Holy Trinity.　The
date of its foundation is not recorded, but it is mentioned
as an hospital in deeds as early as Henry III. ; it then consisted of a master and six brethren.　TANNER states, that
sisters appear to have been admitted at a subsequent period,
who are frequently noticed in old wills.　Before its revenue
fell into disorder, through the mismanagement of "ill-dis-
posed rulers," it enjoyed an ample estate and various immu-
nities.　WEEVER writes, it was a house of great privileges ;
GARDNER adds that it was honoured with masters of good
repute—one an esquire, another a master of arts, etc.　In
TANNER'S time its estates had fallen into decay, the whole
revenues being no more than £13 15s. per annum.　When
GARDNER published his " History of Dunwich," they had
decreased to £11 17s.　Several legacies in old wills were
left to this fabric under the name of Trinity Church.　The
town records say that one named Robert Aleyn, school-
master, had 20s. a year to teach the poor of this establishment.　The gross amounts of lands and tenements in Dunwich is something more than £66 per annum.　In Heven-
ingham they produce £17, and in Ellough £10, making a
total yearly income of about £93.　In 1566, John Page
alias Baxter, by will, gave power to his executors to sell his
estate at Carlton Colville, to the intent that the yearly sum
of £3 should be paid to the town of Dunwich for the poor
thereof; but it is carried to the general account of the
Chamberlains of the Corporation, as part of the private
revenues of that body, without the payment of £3 a year to
the poor.

The following list of the bishops of Dunwich may perhaps not be uninteresting to those readers who are un-
acquainted with its general history :—

Felix, the first bishop, consecrated Anno Dom. 636.

> At Donmoc than was Felix first bishop,
> Of Estangie and taught the Christian faith
> That is full hye in Heven I hope.

　　　　See *Hardynge—Chronicle 'n Metre*, cap. 91.

Thomas, his deacon, succeeded Felix; he was consecrated by Archbishop Honorius, in 647. He was descended from the people called by the Saxons Girvii, who inhabited the counties of Cambridgeshire and Lincolnshire. He governed the See of Dunwich five years.

Bergisel (or Bregilsus, who is also called by historians Bonniface) succeeded him; he held the See seventeen years, and was succeeded in 669, by

Bisa (or Bosa), who was consecrated to his See in the same year by Theodore, archbishop of Canterbury. He "was a very grave and reverend person," but being old and infirm, he was unable to attend to his episcopal duties; he therefore divided his province into two Sees, one remaining at Dunwich, and the other being fixed at North Elmham, in Norfolk. He was present at the council at Hertford, in 673, and died in the same year.

He was succeeded by Etta (or Ecca), who continued in the See at Dunwich about two years, when, with Bedwin, bishop of North-Elmham, he retired to the abbey of St. Osith, and was succeeded by

Astulphus (or Astwolph.) How long this bishop presided in his See is not evident, but it is conjectured that he possessed it not much less than fifty years, as we have no account of his successor.

Endred (GARDNER calls him Ealforth) till the year 731, when Bede concluded his history. Endred was present at the council of Clovesho (or Cliffe) at Hoo in Kent, which was held in the year 747. He subscribed the canons of it by the name of Heardelfus Episcopus Dummocensis.—[See *Spelman Conc. Angl.*, p. 242.]

Cuthwin was the next bishop, and after him

Albert (or Alberth) who was followed by

Eglaff, whose successor was

Heardred. Bishop Godwin says of him, "This is he who is mentioned in the synod with Cuthbert, archbishop of

Canterbury, called in the year 747, which he subscribed by the name of Hardulph." But Wharton, in reference to the time of the meeting of that synod, thinks that it was Eadred above-mentioned, who was bishop of Dunwich at that period.—[See *Wharton's Anglia Sacra.*, vol. i., p. 404.]

Alsin was the twelfth bishop. He died at Sudbury, and was buried at Dunwich.—[See *Gibson's Saxon Chronicle*, p. 68.]

Tedfridus (or Tidferth) was the successor of Alsin. He was bishop of Dunwich when Offa, king of Mercia, made Litchfield an archbishopric, about the year 787. He was present at the synod of Beconfield, in 798; of Clovesho, in 803; and of Celicuth, in the year 813.—[See *Spelman's Concil. Angl.*, p. 318, 325, and 328.]

Weremund was the next bishop; he died in the year 870, He was succeeded by

Wibred (or Wildred), who at the death of Humbert, bishop of Elmham, became possessed of both Sees, which he united, and fixed his episcopal seat at Elmham.

The Almshouses

Were all destroyed before GARDNER's time, from whose history the following notice of them is transcribed :—

> A.D., 1515, September 6th, Test. Petri. Melton. I will that they doo bylde to or fowre housis, as it may be born of my goods, as near the cherch yerd of Saint Peter's aforesaid, as they can purchase any ground therefor.

> 1537, April 1st, T. Petri. Shelly. I will that the east ende of my house callyd Bollyants, shall remaine to an almesse house for poor people to dwell in.

> 1538, January 30th. I wyll that myne executors shall buylde an howse in such place of Dunwich as they shall think that meetest for such poor folkes to dwell in.

> 1556, December 16th, T. Johannis Barnett, Itru. I gyve and bequeth, after my wief's decease, my house and tenemente to the poor people of Dunwiche aforesaid; and that the chamberlains of the said town, for the time beinge, shall let to fearme

the said house to the best profyght, and the money shall comynge to be delte to the said poore people, always at the feast of Ester, and the chamberlaines to have for their pains XII penne.

GARDNER records the generosity of a gentleman, who, before the period of his writing, had allowed twenty pounds a year for a master to instruct and educate the poor children of the town, but which bounty was withholden.

Donewyc, farewell !—While now I gaze alone,
On mouldering tokens of thy glory gone,
I muse on ruthless time, on wind, and sea,
That long have waged unsparing war on thee !
Yes ! —thou art fallen !—and the sea-bird flies
O'er the wild waves where all thy splendour lies !
Thy towering structures which their founders deemed
Almost eternal !—Ha ! they had not dreamed
That all their wondrous strength, their goodly pride
Would fall and waste before the fretting tide !
Thy Forest too, where many a stately oak
Had long withstood time's unrelenting stroke,
Laughed at the storm, defied the thunder's crash,
The whirlwind's fury, and the lightning's flash,
That too is fallen !—and the swelling wave
Rolls in proud triumph o'er its spacious grave !
Sad type of earthly grandeur passed away !
Alas ! the glories of life's transient day,
Man's learning, wisdom, philosophic thought,
His art, power, honor, wealth, desires, are—nought !
Still, Donewyc ! still on thy exalted cliff
I love to pause, to mark the passing skiff
With white and glittering sail, glide softly by,
While Ocean smiles beneath the summer sky,
And whispering breezes from the waveless sea
Come with soft murmurs, while the cheerly bee
Sings her bass song amid the blossomed heath :—
From thy bold heights upon the sea beneath
Oft have I gazed in hours thus calmly bright,
Rapt in a heaven of unalloyed delight !
Scene of my joy, dear object of my song !
I love thy haunts, and I have loved them long ;
Farewell !—farewell !—the bard who sings of thee
Will soon be all that withering man must be,
Low in the dust !—within the silent grave,
No more to hear the murmuring of thy wave,
No more—no more of thee, and thine to tell,
Thou dear, though wild and lonely spot !—Farewell !

In striking contrast with the former greatness of this ancient city we give its present portatiture.

Dunwich is a small borough and parish, bounded on the east by the German Ocean, 5½ miles from Darsham Station, about 3 miles south-by-west from Southwold, and 9 north-east from Saxmundham. The population in 1871 was 234. It still retains its municipal privileges, and is governed by a recorder, two bailiffs (chosen annually), twelve aldermen, twenty-four common councilmen, and two magistrates.

We cannot close our account of this desolated, yet still interesting spot, better than by transcribing the following stanzas from the pages of Suffolk's sweetest bard :—

> Oft gazing on thy craggy brow,
>   We muse on glories over ;
> Fair Dunwich ! thou art lowly now.
>   Renown'd and sought no more.
>
> How proudly rose thy crested seat
>   Above the ocean wave ;
> Yet doomed beneath that sea to meet
>   One wide and sweeping grave.
>
> The stately city greets no more
>   The home-returning bark ;
> Sad relics of her splendour o'er
>   One crumbling spire we mark.
>
> Unlike when ruled by Saxon powers,
>   She sat in ancient pride,
> With all her stately halls and towers,
>   Reflected on the tide.
>
> Those who through each forgotten age
>   With patient care will look,
> Will find her fate in many a page
>   Of Time's extended book.

Lowestoft : G. S. Cook, Nelson Printing Works.

REMARKS ON WORMS
BY
S. F. ABBOTT.

The origin of Worms in the intestinal canal is involved in mystery, although many causes which favour their occurrence are assigned. The water which we drink, the diet, especially if it consists of a large proportion of vegetable aliment ; an excessive use of fruit, sugar, or any other highly nutritous substance ; these have been cited as causes, but perhaps no special origin can be given, unless it be the deprivation of salt, which certainly has appeared in the case of prisoners, punished in this way in Holland, to favour the formation of Worms. Debility, also, from whatever cause arising, undoubtedly favours the generation of these Parasites.

There are several kinds of Worms which infest the alimentary canals of man. Those most generally found are the ASCARIDES, a small Thread Worm, from the eighth of an inch to one and a half inch in length ; they are mostly in the rectum.

The LUMBRICI are long round Worms, from two to ten inches or more in length. They are of a yellowish white colour, and are usually found in the small intestines.

The TÆNIA or Tape Worm is quite the most formidable, and produces the most serious consequences of any of the Intestinal Parasites ; it sometimes grows to many feet in length, extending indeed at times almost throughout the entire length of the intestines.

As may be expected, from the highly organized and sensitive part which they occupy, Worms cause great constitutional derangement, resulting in all kinds of bad symptoms, more especially affecting the stomach and head ; hence we have in these cases variable appetite—sometimes deficient, at others absolutely voracious—pain in the stomach, foetid breath, nausea, head-ache, giddiness, irritation about the nose and arms, frequent cough and disturbed rest, a disordered state of the bowels, epileptic fits, and great emaciation.

Plenty of salt should be eaten with fresh animal food ; yet salt meat is not good for persons troubled with worms.

ABBOTT'S WORM POWDERS
Are an Excellent Vermifuge.

DIRECTIONS.—Half of one of the Powders to be taken at night on going to bed, and half on the following morning. Let one day intervene between their continuance. To be taken in treacle, honey, or preserve.

Prepared and Sold by
S. F. ABBOTT,
TOWN MANSION, LOWESTOFT.
In Packets, 7½d. each. Free by Post for 8 Stamps.
IN ORDERING. PLEASE STATE AGE.

ABBOTT'S
TINCTURE OF LIFE

Is an effectual external Remedy for Paralysis, Sciatica, Rheumatism, Stiff Joints, Pleurisy, Palsy, Lumbago, Catarrh, Tooth-ache, Numbness, Neuralgia, Sprains, Bronchitis, Diptheria, Spinal Diseases, Chilblains, Wasting of the Limbs, and parts that have lost their sensibility.

Remarkable cure of long-standing Rheumatism.

Old House Farm, Beaumont, near Colchester, Essex,

January 23rd, 1871.

Sir.—Excuse the liberty I am taking in writing to you. I must tell you that I have been afflicted with Rheumatism for seven years, so that at times I have not been able to help myself in any way. I have had medical advice, medicine from the best of doctors, and even from Apothecaries' Hall has medicine been brought me, beside a month's stay in London, on purpose to be under the treatment of one of the head physicians.

A friend of mine brought me a bottle of your "TINCTURE OE LIFE." I can sincerely say that it has done for me what all the doctors and physiciaus failed to do I can now walk with ease and pleasure, and free from pain. I wish I could get every one afflicted with Rheumatism to use it ; I am sure it would do them good. I shall be pleased for you to use my testimonial.

I am, yours respectfully,

To Mr. S. F. ABBOTT.　　　　　　　　　　　　　　　　　M. A. ADAMS.
Town Mansion, Lowestoft.

S. F. ABBOTT,
TOWN MANSION, HIGH ST., LOWESTOFT.

Sold also by SANGER & SONS, BARCLAY & SONS, EDWARDS & SONS, London,
and by all Chemists,

In Bottles, 9d, 1/1½, and 2/9 each.

DIRECTIONS.

Procure a piece of flannel, which when folded in two is sufficiently large to bind on the part affected. Moisten the flannel with the Tincture, and well rub wherever pain is felt. Add more Tincture to the flannel, and secure it to the most painful part The flannel must be worn until the disease is removed. Every day add fresh Tincture.

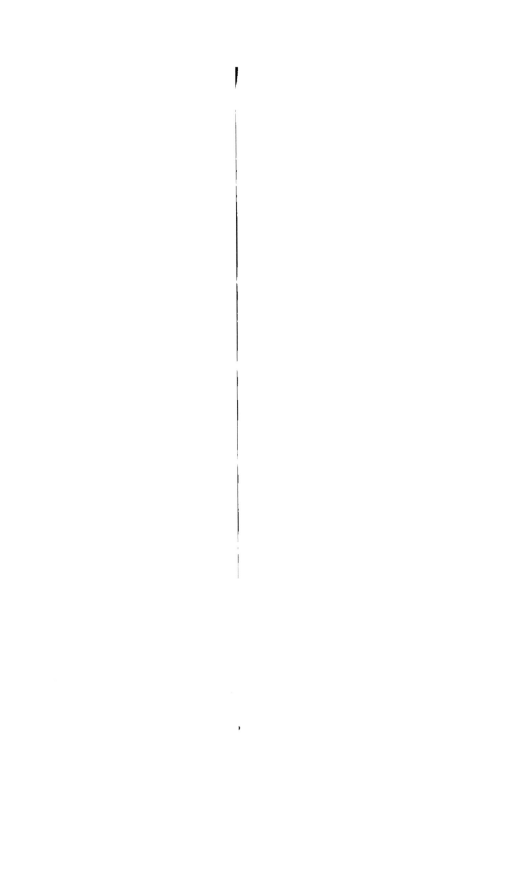